The 90-Day Gratitude Journal
A Mindful Practice for Lifetime of Happiness

by

S.J. Scott

Barrie Davenport

Why the World Needs More Gratitude

Do you often feel surrounded by negativity?

Every day, we are bombarded by bad news, political discord, and catastrophic world events.

If those weren't enough, our inboxes and social media feeds are cluttered with updates on the newest disease that will kill us, advertisements for products we should buy to feel happy, and all the reasons we aren't attractive, wealthy, or successful enough.

We constantly deal with negativity, yet we are weirdly addicted to the information that is feeding our inner angst and unhappiness.

But if you turned off the television, shut down your phone, and closed the lid on your computer, life wouldn't seem so bad, would it?

You have most of what you need and a lot of what you want in life. There are good things happening all around you. People love you. There's food on the table. You have a bed to sleep in and a roof over your head.

The antidote to our unhappiness isn't the newest thing, the latest diet fad, or the next achievement.

The antidote is gratitude.

Gratitude for what you have right now. Gratitude for the people in your life. Gratitude for all good things that are available to you in this moment.

Being grateful isn't an idea you stick on a Post-It note for a quick shot of feel-good. There's a reason (many reasons, in fact) why you are hearing it touted so much.

Gratitude can transform you. It can pull you from the vortex of negativity that is sucking the life out of you, and give you a renewed sense of purpose and joy.

And the simplest way to practice gratitude is to turn it into a daily habit—specifically through the book you're holding right now: *The 90-Day Gratitude Journal: A Mindful Practice for Lifetime of Happiness*.

The 90-Day Gratitude Journal is your personal tool for injecting a dose of positivity into your day. You can use it to focus your attention on what is going right in your life instead of focusing on everything that's going wrong.

You can use it to pause for a few minutes every day and truly appreciate all that you have.

If you make the commitment to complete the entire journal, you'll have a diary of all the wonderful things that you can be thankful for. Whenever you feel frustrated or anxious, you can review this journal and recognize that life is pretty good.

Okay, are you ready to dive in?

Let's talk about the nine benefits of practicing gratitude.

9 Benefits of Practicing Gratitude

Still unsure about *how* gratitude can help you? Here are nine ways that gratitude will lead to improvements in both your psychological and physical well-being.

#1. Gratitude increases your happiness.

When you regularly practice gratitude, you'll start to notice that you're surround by an abundance of positivity. These are the things that you may have taken for granted in the past. But when you learn to truly appreciate them, your levels of happiness will increase.

This increase in happiness has been supported by two studies.

First, according to an article in the Harvard Healthy Newsletter [1], which outlines research on the topic, "Gratitude is strongly and consistently associated with greater happiness. Gratitude helps people feel more positive emotions, relish good experiences, improve their health, deal with adversity, and build strong relationships."

Also, Martin Seligman and his team performed a study [2] where they asked participants to write down "three good things" that occurred during their day, with an explanation of why each item was personally important.

After completing this exercise for a week, the participants reported more happiness (and less depression) at
the one-month, three-month, and six-month follow-up
sessions.

In short, gratitude makes you happier because you de-
velop an appreciation for everything positive in your life
instead of taking it for granted.

#2. Gratitude improves your mental health.
If you're tired of feeling anxious, dissatisfied, frustrated,
and depressed, then gratitude can be the key to reduc-
ing stress and depression.

In her book *The How of Happiness* [3], researcher and
psychologist Dr. Sonja Lyubomirsky states, "Gratitude is
an antidote to negative emotions, a neutralizer of envy,
hostility, worry, and irritation. It is savoring; it is not taking
things for granted; it is present oriented."

#3. Gratitude helps you savor positive experiences.
We all have our favorite memories. Maybe they include
meeting your spouse or partner, seeing the birth of
your child (or children), celebrating big milestones or
achievements, or taking the vacation of a lifetime.

Unfortunately, once those experiences have come and gone, we rarely take the time to think about how amazing they were. Even when good things happen, we are often so distracted that we don't fully experience the joy of that moment.

By being engaged in the present moment, you will gain appreciation from every experience. Just reminding yourself to stop and feel grateful gives you a boost and enhances the richness of the occasion.

#4. Gratitude helps you cope with major life challenges.

Trauma, stress, and negative life events can have the counterintuitive effect of making us feel more grateful.

In his book *Thanks! How Practicing Gratitude Can Make You Happier* [4], Dr. Robert Emmon found that in the days after the 9/11 attacks in the U.S., gratitude was the second most commonly felt emotion after sympathy.

According to Emmon, "People might have felt grateful to be alive or to know that their loved ones were safe."

All the positive things in our lives come into sharp focus when something tragic happens to us or around us. When we deal with stress or adversity, gratitude helps us cope and process our emotions in a healthy way.

By focusing on the positive aspects of our lives rather than allowing ourselves to be overwhelmed by negative events, we feel more in control and optimistic about our situation.

#5. Gratitude fosters resilience.

When you are grateful for what you have, you are better able to overcome negative events in your life. You don't view your life as a "glass half empty," but rather you recognize that despite bad things happening, you will survive, and even thrive.

In fact, gratefulness was shown to be a critical factor in preventing post-traumatic stress disorder in veterans after the Vietnam War, and following the terrorist attacks on 9/11.

With the practice of gratitude, you build your inner coping muscle, allowing you to manage life's difficulties with less emotional trauma.

#6. Gratitude boosts your self-esteem.

Practicing gratitude allows you to reflect on your achievements, the important people in your life, and the blessings you encounter every day. By focusing on these things, you're able to see how much you have done to make good things happen.

Your hard work has resulted in the house you live in and the material things you own.

Your love, devotion, and presence have helped build a strong and secure family.

Your efforts in school and past jobs have landed you in this career.

Expressing gratitude for all your own skills, interests, and achievements will boost your feelings of self-worth.

#7. Gratitude fosters empathy.

Gratitude inspires you to be less materialistic and more inclined to help others. As you focus on your own blessings, you become keenly aware of what other people *don't* have.

When you feel grateful for easy access to food and water, you might be inspired to help someone who doesn't. As you express gratefulness for your wonderful friendships, you might decide to reach out to someone who is lonely.

The practice of gratitude has a spillover effect, making you more aware of the feelings and suffering of others long after you practice it. You become a more compassionate person in general.

#8. Gratitude gives you a better night's sleep.

Do you often lie in bed wide-eyed, worrying about your problems? If so, a simple way to remove your anxieties is to practice gratitude before bedtime.

In fact, one study [5] found that gratitude journaling before bed can reduce worry and pessimism, helping you relax and fall asleep faster. Some study participants reported getting longer, more refreshing sleep as well.

#9. Gratitude strengthens relationships.

Do you want a happier, stronger marriage? Focus on your partner's good qualities and the positive aspects of your relationship, rather than dwelling on what's missing.

- **Do you want closer friendships?** Let your friends know how much you appreciate them, and how grateful you are to have them as friends.

- **Do you want more success at work?** Tell your boss and coworkers how thankful you are for their support and hard work.

- You don't even need to tell people you're grateful (although it's a nice thing to do) in order to benefit. Just *feeling* gratitude for these people will improve your relationships with them.

Gratitude strengthens feelings of intimacy and connectedness with others. The closer you feel with the important people in your life, the more you will discover and enjoy about them—which in turn gives you more to feel grateful about.

Having close, satisfying relationships is a huge factor in lifelong happiness and health.

As you can see, you'll enjoy many benefits by regularly practicing gratitude. Now let's talk about how to incorporate this habit into your busy schedule.

How to Build
the Gratitude Journaling Habit

It's not hard to create the gratitude journaling habit. All you have to do is schedule this activity and use simple habit-building strategies to make sure you never miss a day.

Both authors (Steve "S.J." Scott & Barrie Davenport) talk extensively about creating habits on their websites, but for now, here's an overview of the simple seven-step process.

Step #1: Focus on Building Just the Gratitude Habit

One common mistake is trying to build multiple habits at the same time. This problem relates to "**ego depletion**," which is a person's "diminished capacity to regulate their thoughts, feelings, and actions," according to the book *Willpower*, by Roy F. Baumeister and John Tierney [6].

Our willpower is like a muscle. It weakens throughout the day because of constant use. You use your willpower when you make dozens of decisions each day. You use your willpower to concentrate at work. You use willpower to resist eating junk food. And you use willpower to resist lashing out at others when you're tired from a long day of work.

Because of ego depletion, your ability to form new habits is limited since there are only so many "new" things your willpower can handle at once. To keep things easy, we <u>strongly recommend</u> that you work on building *just* the gratitude practice for the next month, increasing the likelihood that you'll make this habit stick!

Step #2: Commit to Thirty (or More) Days of Gratitude

Gratitude will help you gain a new appreciation for life. But this doesn't mean it will be a simple or quick process. In fact, it might take you a few attempts to turn journaling into permanent behavior.

Some people say it takes twenty-one days to build a habit, while others claim it takes up to sixty-six days. The truth is that the length of time varies from person to person and from habit to habit. You'll find that some habits are easy to build, while others require more effort. Our advice is to commit to gratitude for the next thirty days *at a minimum*.

We recommend that you schedule a daily block of time of at least five to ten minutes to write in this journal.

Step #3: Anchor Gratitude to an Established Habit

Practicing gratitude *shouldn't* be based upon motivation, fads, or temporary desire. Rather, it should be integrated in your life in a way that allows the behavior to become automatic. To do this, you don't need a series of sophisticated steps—just a simple strategy you can commit to, day in and day out, without fail.

We suggest that you "anchor" the gratitude journaling practice to habits that you *already* do daily. These habits should be automatic on your part—like eating, sleeping, or going to the bathroom. You wouldn't forget to complete any of these actions, so by attaching your gratitude habit to one of them, you won't forget to perform it.

When anchoring, your goal is to practice gratitude before or after you complete one of these habits:

- Drinking your first cup of tea (or coffee) in the morning.
- When your alarm clock goes off.
- When you get into bed in the evening (you can also create a visual cue by leaving this journal on your nightstand).
- Before or after you finish a specific meal (breakfast, lunch, or dinner).

- When you walk into a specific room for the first time (e.g., your den or home office).

There are countless options for picking an established habit. The trick is to identify an action you do every single day and attach gratitude journaling to it. When you pick the *right* habit, you'll discover that it's not hard to turn gratitude into an automatic behavior.

Step #4: Track the Gratitude Habit

It's not enough to anchor gratitude to another habit—you also need a mechanism to reinforce this behavior daily.

The simplest tool for building reinforcement is your mobile phone (since it's a device most people have on them throughout the day). We suggest that you install one of three apps, and use it to create reminders for practicing the gratitude habit.

- **Strides (http://www.stridesapp.com)**: Strides has a clean, simple interface that allows you to track all your habits and goals. It's currently the app that Steve uses to manages all his personal habits.
- **Coach.me (https://www.coach.me)**: This is another great tool. Not only can you use it to stick to your habits, you can also connect with a coach to help

you build a specific habit.

- **Chains (https://chains.cc)**: Chains is built on Jerry Seinfeld's "never break the chain" concept [7], where you commit to a specific habit and never miss a day, creating a chain of positive behaviors in your life.

Finally, if you're not interested in downloading a whole new app, then you can also set a reminder to practice gratitude using one of these popular tools:

- Google Calendar (https://calendar.google.com)
- Evernote (https://evernote.com)
- Todoist (https://todoist.com)

Regardless of the tool you pick, we recommend keeping track of your gratitude journaling habit by using some type of tool. You'll be surprised at how often the behavior of "checking in" makes the difference between whether you do or do not practice gratitude for the day.

Step #5: Plan for Potential Obstacles

With any new habit, you'll face obstacles—even gratitude journaling. While this practice might seem simple to complete, there *will be* those days when it seems impossible to carve out an extra 5-10 minutes.

You'll probably encounter obstacles like:

- Not having enough time.
- Feeling too self-conscious with certain prompts.
- Forgetting to pack *The 90-Day Gratitude Journal* for a vacation.
- Feeling too angry (or sad, upset, stressed, etc.) to practice gratitude.
- Struggling to think of unique ways to express gratitude.

The key to overcoming (or even preventing) these obstacles is recognizing that they happen to all of us. Once you do, you can create a specific plan for how you'll handle each of the challenges that you frequently experience.

We recommend you create "if-then statements" for the actions you'll take when certain challenges arise.

Here are a few examples:

- "If I keep forgetting to practice gratitude, then I will schedule this habit for earlier in the day where I have more time."
- "If I can't think of anything to be grateful for when journaling, I'll write down ideas as they come to me throughout the day."
- "If I have a bad day and don't feel in the mood to journal, then I will simply focus on trying to find just

<u>one</u> positive thing to write about."

- "If I forget my journal, then I will keep a list of reasons to be grateful on my cell phone, and update the journal when it's available."
- "If I find myself stressed or angry at the world, then I will pause for a few seconds to look for something positive about how I'm currently feeling."

When you have a plan, you can overcome any obstacle that comes your way, and know how you'll respond to each situation.

Step #6: Practice Gratitude Throughout the Day

One the key strategies for habit development is taking small steps when building new behaviors, and we've designed *The 90-Day Gratitude Journal* to be as easy as possible. Each day, you'll respond to three simple prompts, which take no more than ten minutes to complete.

That said, to gain the full benefit of gratitude, you should consider practicing throughout the day—especially when you're anxious or stressed. That's why we invite you to practice gratitude whenever you:

- Feel anger at an insignificant event.
- Get annoyed during a daily commute.

- Get into an argument with an important person in your life.
- Are enjoying a small moment with a friend or family member.
- Encounter a particularly challenging obstacle.
- Are using a piece of technology that is frustrating you.

There are countless ways to experience gratitude in your life. The trick is to pause for a few seconds and think about what is wonderful at that very moment.

Step #7: Reward Yourself for Consistency

Practicing gratitude should be a rewarding experience. Not only can you gain an appreciation for what's great in your life, you can also create a reward system based on the number of days you've successfully practiced this behavior.

For example, you could reward yourself whenever you hit important milestones. You could:

- Go see a movie after practicing gratitude for one week.
- Enjoy a date night out with your significant other after a month.

- Go on a weekend getaway after six months of gratitude.
- Splurge on an expensive treat after a year.

You get the picture.

Really, the rewards themselves don't matter. What's important is creating positive reinforcement for practicing gratitude every single day.

If you get stuck, we recommend reading Steve's article that covers 155 ways to reward yourself: https://www.developgoodhabits.com/reward-yourself/

Now that you understand why gratitude is important, and how to turn it into a daily habit, so let's go over the three prompts that are included in this journal so you can get started *writing* in it.

How to Use
The 90-Day Gratitude Journal

In this 90-day journal, you'll answer three questions, which won't take more than ten minutes of your time. Two of the prompts will be the same every day, but the third will be a "wild card" question that challenges you to think about a specific aspect of your life.

Let's go over each of the three prompts and why they're important.

> **Question 1:** "I am grateful for _____, because _____."

This question is based on a study by Martin Seligman [8] that confirmed that the best way to express gratitude is to not only describe what you're grateful for, but also to take the time to consider the actions that led to this good result. When you start to see a positive correlation between your actions and certain events, you'll do more to attract these good things into your life.

The purpose here is to challenge you to be ultra-specific about what you're *currently* grateful for. This means you'll describe how a person, event, or item has benefited your life, and in what ways you have been helped.

There are many things to be grateful for:

- *Specific people in your life.* Even with someone who annoys or angers you, there is always a lesson to be learned from every interaction you have with others.

- *Certain possessions.* You can journal about items that have enriched your life or made it better in some way.

- *Things you take for granted.* There are many people, possessions, or conditions in your life right now that you might take for granted—like your health, job, relationships, or even a piece of technology. A great way to express gratitude is to recognize how your life would be different if you didn't have one of these specific items.

- *Random surprises.* One of the best ways to feel grateful is by taking the time to recognize the unexpected, positive events that occur.

- *Small moments.* Sometimes the best things to be grateful for are those everyday experiences. Playing with your children. A warm summer day. The taste of your favorite beverage. Taking time to appreciate these moments will help you value every single experience.

To show how this prompt works, here is an item that Steve journaled about recently:

> "I am grateful for the 1812 *Overture* by Pyotr
> Tchaikovsky, because listening to it
> at the end of my run got me through
> those difficult last two miles."

Sure, this might seem like a small thing to be grateful for, but that's the idea—you should constantly look at the world around you and acknowledge all that's wonderful in your life.

Finally, we challenge you to come up with a unique answer for every day you journal. That way, you'll have an ongoing list of all the items and people that have added value to your existence. You can then review this journal whenever you feel the need for an emotional boost.

Question #2:
"What am I looking forward to today (or tomorrow)?"

This question should be easy to answer.

If you're journaling in the morning, write down one thing that you're looking forward to doing by the end of the day. It could be spending time with someone important, working on a fun project, or simply relaxing at the end of the day.

If you prefer to journal in the evening, then journal about something you're excited about for tomorrow.

Don't overthink your response here. Just pick one thing that will be wonderful about the next 24 hours.

Question #3: Unique, specific questions.

The last question is a "wild card" prompt. Each day, you will be asked a unique question about an aspect of your life.

We cover a variety of topics with this question, including specific people in your life, favorite memories, challenges you've overcome, and common items you've taken for granted.

Also, on every 10th day, the prompt will ask you to list ten responses to a simple question related to gratitude. For question #3, we challenge you to write as much information as you'd like. We have provided a half page of white space where you can journal a detailed response. Feel free to put as much (or as little) as you'd like in this section.

That's a brief overview of the three questions you'll find within the journal. Let's begin your gratitude journey by starting with Day 1.

DAY 1

DATE ____/____/____

> When you are grateful, fear disappears and abundance appears.
>
> — TONY ROBBINS

Question #1: "I am grateful for_____, because _____."

_____

_____

_____

Question #2: "What am I looking forward to today (or tomorrow)?"

_____

_____

_____

Question #3: Describe your happiest childhood memory.

_____

_____

_____

_____

_____

_____

_____

_____

_____

DAY 2

DATE ____/____/____

> *Act with kindness, but do not expect gratitude.*
>
> — CONFUCIUS

Question #1: "I am grateful for_____, because _____."

_____

_____

_____

Question #2: "What am I looking forward to today (or tomorrow)?"

_____

_____

_____

Question #3: What is a popular song that you enjoy (and why do you like it)?

_____

_____

_____

_____

_____

_____

_____

_____

DAY 3

DATE ____/____/____

> *Develop an attitude of gratitude. Say thank you to everyone you meet for everything they do for you.*
>
> — BRIAN TRACY

Question #1: "I am grateful for_____, because _____."

_____

_____

_____

Question #2: "What am I looking forward to today (or tomorrow)?"

_____

_____

_____

Question #3: What is one of your favorite songs from your childhood?

_____

_____

_____

_____

_____

_____

_____

_____

DAY 4

DATE ____/ ____/ ____

> *An attitude of gratitude brings great things.*
>
> — YOGI BHAJAN

Question #1: "I am grateful for_____, because _____."

_____

_____

_____

Question #2: "What am I looking forward to today (or tomorrow)?"

_____

_____

_____

Question #3: Who is the one friend you can always rely on?

_____

_____

_____

_____

_____

_____

_____

_____

_____

DAY 5

DATE ____/____/____

> *Stop now. Enjoy the moment. It's now or never.*
>
> — MAXIME LAGACÉ

Question #1: "I am grateful for_____, because _____."

_____

_____

_____

Question #2: "What am I looking forward to today (or tomorrow)?"

_____

_____

_____

Question #3: What is the biggest accomplishment in your personal life?

_____

_____

_____

_____

_____

_____

_____

_____

DAY 6

DATE ____/____/____

Question #1: "I am grateful for_____, because _____."

_____

_____

_____

Question #2: "What am I looking forward to today (or tomorrow)?"

_____

_____

_____

Question #3: What is the biggest accomplishment in your professional life?

_____

_____

_____

_____

_____

_____

_____

_____

DAY 7

DATE ____/____/____

> *The essence of all beautiful art is gratitude.*
>
> — FRIEDRICH NIETZCHE

Question #1: "I am grateful for_____, because _____."

_____

_____

_____

Question #2: "What am I looking forward to today (or tomorrow)?"

_____

_____

_____

Question #3: What is your favorite memory of your father (or stepfather)?

_____

_____

_____

_____

_____

_____

_____

_____

DAY 8

DATE ____/____/____

> The smallest act of kindness is worth more than the grandest intention.
>
> — OSCAR WILDE

Question #1: "I am grateful for_____, because _____."

_____

_____

_____

Question #2: "What am I looking forward to today (or tomorrow)?"

_____

_____

_____

Question #3: What is your favorite memory of your mother (or stepmother)?

_____

_____

_____

_____

_____

_____

_____

_____

DAY 9

DATE ____/____/____

> *No duty is more urgent than that of returning thanks.*
>
> — JAMES ALLEN

Question #1: "I am grateful for_____, because _____."

_____

_____

_____

Question #2: "What am I looking forward to today (or tomorrow)?"

_____

_____

_____

Question #3: Describe your favorite pet (or former pet)?

_____

_____

_____

_____

_____

_____

_____

_____

_____

DAY 10

DATE ____/____/____

> *Gratitude changes everything.*
>
> — ANONYMOUS

Question #1: "I am grateful for_____, because _____."

_____

_____

_____

Question #2: "What am I looking forward to today (or tomorrow)?"

_____

_____

_____

Question #3: List 10 hobbies and activities that bring you joy?

_____

_____

_____

_____

_____

_____

_____

_____

DAY 11

DATE ____/____/____

> *Gratitude makes sense of your past, brings peace for today, and creates a vision for tomorrow.*
>
> — MELODY BEATTIE

Question #1: "I am grateful for_____, because _____."

_____

_____

_____

Question #2: "What am I looking forward to today (or tomorrow)?"

_____

_____

_____

Question #3: What is a mistake that you've made and that ultimately led to a positive experience?

_____

_____

_____

_____

_____

_____

_____

_____

DAY 12

DATE ____/____/____

> *The highest tribute to the dead is not grief but gratitude.*
>
> — THORNTON WILDER

Question #1: "I am grateful for_____, because _____."

_____

_____

_____

Question #2: "What am I looking forward to today (or tomorrow)?"

_____

_____

_____

Question #3: Describe a family tradition that you are most grateful for.

_____

_____

_____

_____

_____

_____

_____

_____

DAY 13

DATE ____/____/____

> *True forgiveness is when you can say, Thank you for that experience.*
>
> — OPRAH WINFREY

Question #1: "I am grateful for_____, because _____."

_____

_____

_____

Question #2: "What am I looking forward to today (or tomorrow)?"

_____

_____

_____

Question #3: Who is a teacher or mentor that has made an impact on your life, and how did they help you?

_____

_____

_____

_____

_____

_____

_____

_____

DAY 14

DATE ____/____/____

> *Nothing new can come into your life unless you are grateful for what you already have.*
>
> — MICHAEL BERNHARD

Question #1: "I am grateful for_____, because _____."

_____

_____

_____

Question #2: "What am I looking forward to today (or tomorrow)?"

_____

_____

_____

Question #3: What do you like the most about your town or city?

_____

_____

_____

_____

_____

_____

_____

_____

DAY 15

DATE ____/____/____

> *Appreciation is a wonderful thing: It makes what is excellent in others belong to us as well.*
>
> — VOLTAIRE

Question #1: "I am grateful for_____, because _____."

_____

_____

_____

Question #2: "What am I looking forward to today (or tomorrow)?"

_____

_____

_____

Question #3: Describe your favorite location in your house and why you like it.

_____

_____

_____

_____

_____

_____

_____

_____

DAY 16

DATE ____/____/____

> *There is always something to be grateful for.*
>
> — ANONYMOUS

Question #1: "I am grateful for_____, because _____."

_____

_____

_____

Question #2: "What am I looking forward to today (or tomorrow)?"

_____

_____

_____

Question #3: What is one thing you've learned this week that you're thankful for?

_____

_____

_____

_____

_____

_____

_____

_____

DAY 17

DATE ____/____/____

Nothing is more honorable than a grateful heart.

— LUCIUS ANNAEUS SENECA

Question #1: "I am grateful for_____, because _____."

_____

_____

_____

Question #2: "What am I looking forward to today (or tomorrow)?"

_____

_____

_____

Question #3: Who made you smile in the past 24 hours and why?

_____

_____

_____

_____

_____

_____

_____

_____

DAY 18

DATE ____/____/____

> *Gratitude; my cup over floweth.*
>
> — OSCAR WILDE

Question #1: "I am grateful for_____, because _____."

_____

_____

_____

Question #2: "What am I looking forward to today (or tomorrow)?"

_____

_____

_____

Question #3: What is a recent purchase that has added value to your life?

_____

_____

_____

_____

_____

_____

_____

_____

DAY 19

DATE ____ / ____ / ____

> *Hope has a good memory, gratitude a bad one.*
>
> — BALTASAR GRACIAN

Question #1: "I am grateful for_____, because _____."

_____

_____

_____

Question #2: "What am I looking forward to today (or tomorrow)?"

_____

_____

_____

Question #3: What is biggest lesson you learned in child-hood?

_____

_____

_____

_____

_____

_____

_____

_____

DAY 20

> *There are always flowers for those who want to see them.*
>
> — HENRI MATISSE

Question #1: "I am grateful for_____, because _____."

_____

_____

_____

Question #2: "What am I looking forward to today (or tomorrow)?"

_____

_____

_____

Question #3: List 10 ways you can share your gratitude with other people in the next 24 hours.

_____

_____

_____

_____

_____

_____

_____

_____

DAY 21

> *Happiness is itself a kind of gratitude.*
>
> — ANONYMOUS

Question #1: "I am grateful for_____, because _____."

_____

_____

_____

Question #2: "What am I looking forward to today (or tomorrow)?"

_____

_____

_____

Question #3: Describe your favorite smell.

_____

_____

_____

_____

_____

_____

_____

_____

_____

DAY 22

> *Living in a state of gratitude is the gateway to grace.*
>
> — ARIANNA HUFFINGTON

Question #1: "I am grateful for_____, because _____."

_____

_____

_____

Question #2: "What am I looking forward to today (or tomorrow)?"

_____

_____

_____

Question #3: Describe your favorite sound.

_____

_____

_____

_____

_____

_____

_____

_____

_____

DAY 23

DATE ____/____/____

> *My day begins and ends with gratitude.*
>
> — LOUISE HAY

Question #1: "I am grateful for_____, because _____."

_____

_____

_____

Question #2: "What am I looking forward to today (or tomorrow)?"

_____

_____

_____

Question #3: Describe your favorite sight.

_____

_____

_____

_____

_____

_____

_____

_____

_____

DAY 24

DATE _____/_____/_____

> *Walk as if you are kissing the earth with your feet.*
>
> — THICH NHAT HANH

Question #1: "I am grateful for_____, because _____."

_____

_____

_____

Question #2: "What am I looking forward to today (or tomorrow)?"

_____

_____

_____

Question #3: Describe your favorite taste.

_____

_____

_____

_____

_____

_____

_____

_____

DAY 25

DATE ____/____/____

> *Things must be felt with the heart.*
>
> — HELEN KELLER

Question #1: "I am grateful for_____, because _____."

_____

_____

_____

Question #2: "What am I looking forward to today (or tomorrow)?"

_____

_____

_____

Question #3: Describe your favorite sensation.

_____

_____

_____

_____

_____

_____

_____

_____

_____

DAY 26

DATE ____/____/____

> *Forget injuries, never forget kindnesses.*
>
> — CONFUCIUS

Question #1: "I am grateful for_____, because _____."

_____

_____

_____

Question #2: "What am I looking forward to today (or tomorrow)?"

_____

_____

_____

Question #3: How can you pamper yourself in the next 24 hours?

_____

_____

_____

_____

_____

_____

_____

_____

DAY 27

DATE ____/ ____/ ____

> *Thank you is the best prayer that anyone could say. I say that one a lot. Thank you expresses extreme gratitude, humility, understanding.*
>
> — ALICE WALKER

Question #1: "I am grateful for_____, because _____."

_____

_____

_____

Question #2: "What am I looking forward to today (or tomorrow)?"

_____

_____

_____

Question #3: Name and write about someone you've never met but who has helped your life in some way.

_____

_____

_____

_____

_____

_____

_____

DAY 28

DATE ____/____/____

> *Gratitude is the fairest blossom that springs from the soul.*
>
> — HENRY WARD BEECHER

Question #1: "I am grateful for_____, because _____."

_____

_____

_____

Question #2: "What am I looking forward to today (or tomorrow)?"

_____

_____

_____

Question #3: How is your life more positive today than it was a year ago?

_____

_____

_____

_____

_____

_____

_____

DAY 29

DATE ____/____/____

> *Gratitude is riches. Complaint is poverty.*
>
> — DORIS DAY

Question #1: "I am grateful for_____, because _____."

_____

_____

_____

Question #2: "What am I looking forward to today (or tomorrow)?"

_____

_____

_____

Question #3: What do other people like about you?

_____

_____

_____

_____

_____

_____

_____

_____

_____

_____

DAY 30

DATE ____/____/____

> So much has been given to me; I have no time to ponder over that which has been denied.
>
> — HELEN KELLER

Question #1: "I am grateful for_____, because _____."

_____

_____

_____

Question #2: "What am I looking forward to today (or tomorrow)?"

_____

_____

_____

Question #3: List 10 skills you have that most people don't possess.

_____

_____

_____

_____

_____

_____

_____

_____

DAY 31

DATE ____/____/____

Question #1: "I am grateful for_____, because _____."

_____

_____

_____

Question #2: "What am I looking forward to today (or tomorrow)?"

_____

_____

_____

Question #3: Describe the last time someone helped you solve a problem at work.

_____

_____

_____

_____

_____

_____

_____

_____

DAY 32

> *If you want to find happiness, find gratitude.*
>
> — STEVE MARABOLI

Question #1: "I am grateful for_____, because _____."

_____

_____

_____

Question #2: "What am I looking forward to today (or tomorrow)?"

_____

_____

_____

Question #3: What is your favorite part of your daily routine?

_____

_____

_____

_____

_____

_____

_____

_____

DAY 33

DATE ____/____/____

> *Silent gratitude isn't very much use to anyone.*
>
> — GERTRUDE STEIN

Question #1: "I am grateful for_____, because _____."

_____

_____

_____

Question #2: "What am I looking forward to today (or tomorrow)?"

_____

_____

_____

Question #3: What is a great book you've recently read?

_____

_____

_____

_____

_____

_____

_____

_____

_____

DAY 34

DATE ____/____/____

> *The roots of all goodness lie in the soil of appreciation for goodness.*
>
> — DALAI LAMA

Question #1: "I am grateful for_____, because _____."

_____

_____

_____

Question #2: "What am I looking forward to today (or tomorrow)?"

_____

_____

_____

Question #3: What is your favorite holiday, and why do you love it?

_____

_____

_____

_____

_____

_____

_____

_____

DAY 35

DATE ____/____/____

> *Gratitude is the sign of noble souls.*
>
> — AESOP

Question #1: "I am grateful for_____, because _____."

_____

_____

_____

Question #2: "What am I looking forward to today (or tomorrow)?"

_____

_____

_____

Question #3: What is your favorite TV show, and why do you love it?

_____

_____

_____

_____

_____

_____

_____

_____

DAY 36

> *Every blessing ignored becomes a curse.*
>
> — PAULO COELHO

Question #1: "I am grateful for_____, because _____."

_____

_____

_____

Question #2: "What am I looking forward to today (or tomorrow)?"

_____

_____

_____

Question #3: What is your favorite movie, and why do you love it?

_____

_____

_____

_____

_____

_____

_____

_____

DAY 37

> *Through the eyes of gratitude, everything is a miracle.*
>
> — MARY DAVIS

Question #1: "I am grateful for_____, because _____."

_____

_____

_____

Question #2: "What am I looking forward to today (or tomorrow)?"

_____

_____

_____

Question #3: What is your favorite way to enjoy nature (e.g., walking in the woods, sitting on the beach, hiking in the mountains, etc.)?

_____

_____

_____

_____

_____

_____

_____

DAY 38

DATE ____/____/____

> *This a wonderful day. I've never seen this one before.*
>
> — MAYA ANGELOU

Question #1: "I am grateful for_____, because _____."

_____

_____

_____

Question #2: "What am I looking forward to today (or tomorrow)?"

_____

_____

_____

Question #3: Write about a recent obstacle you faced and how you overcame it.

_____

_____

_____

_____

_____

_____

_____

_____

DAY 39

DATE ____/____/____

> *The real gift of gratitude is that the more grateful you are,*
> *the more present you become.*
>
> — ROBERT HOLDEN

Question #1: "I am grateful for_____, because _____."

_____

_____

_____

Question #2: "What am I looking forward to today (or tomorrow)?"

_____

_____

_____

Question #3: Describe a favorite pet and what you love(d) about it.

_____

_____

_____

_____

_____

_____

_____

_____

DAY 40

DATE ____/____/____

> *If you are really thankful, what do you do? You share.*
>
> — W. CLEMENT STONE

Question #1: "I am grateful for_____, because _____."

_____

_____

_____

Question #2: "What am I looking forward to today (or tomorrow)?"

_____

_____

_____

Question #3: List 10 things you are looking forward to in the next year.

_____

_____

_____

_____

_____

_____

_____

_____

DAY 41

DATE ____/____/____

> *Three meals plus bedtime make four sure blessings a day.*
>
> — MASON COOLEY

Question #1: "I am grateful for_____, because _____."

_____

_____

_____

Question #2: "What am I looking forward to today (or tomorrow)?"

_____

_____

_____

Question #3: What do you love most about your country?

_____

_____

_____

_____

_____

_____

_____

_____

_____

DAY 42

DATE ____/____/____

> Gratitude is the most exquisite form of courtesy.
>
> — JACQUES MARITAIN

Question #1: "I am grateful for_____, because _____."

_____

_____

_____

Question #2: "What am I looking forward to today (or tomorrow)?"

_____

_____

_____

Question #3: What is your favorite food you love to indulge in?

_____

_____

_____

_____

_____

_____

_____

_____

DAY 43

DATE ____/____/____

> *The struggle ends when gratitude begins.*
>
> — NEALE DONALD WALSCH

Question #1: "I am grateful for_____, because _____."

_____

_____

_____

Question #2: "What am I looking forward to today (or tomorrow)?"

_____

_____

_____

Question #3: Write about someone who makes your life better.

_____

_____

_____

_____

_____

_____

_____

_____

DAY 44

DATE ____/ ____/ ____

> *When we give cheerfully and accept gratefully, everyone is blessed.*
>
> — MAYA ANGELOU

Question #1: "I am grateful for_____, because _____."

_____

_____

_____

Question #2: "What am I looking forward to today (or tomorrow)?"

_____

_____

_____

Question #3: If you're single, what is your favorite part about being single? Or if you're married, what is your favorite part about being married?

_____

_____

_____

_____

_____

_____

_____

DAY 45

DATE ____/____/____

> *Don't pray when it rains if you don't pray when the sun shines.*
>
> — LEROY SATCHEL PAIGE

Question #1: "I am grateful for_____, because _____."

_____

_____

_____

Question #2: "What am I looking forward to today (or tomorrow)?"

_____

_____

_____

Question #3: What is today's weather, and what is one positive thing you can say about it?

_____

_____

_____

_____

_____

_____

_____

_____

DAY 46

DATE ___/___/___

> Gratitude opens the door to the power, the wisdom, the creativity of the universe. You open the door through gratitude.
>
> — DEEPAK CHOPRA

Question #1: "I am grateful for_____, because _____."

_____

_____

_____

Question #2: "What am I looking forward to today (or tomorrow)?"

_____

_____

_____

Question #3: Describe a weird family tradition that you love.

_____

_____

_____

_____

_____

_____

_____

DAY 47

> *May you wake with gratitude.*
>
> — ANONYMOUS

Question #1: "I am grateful for_____, because _____."

_____

_____

_____

Question #2: "What am I looking forward to today (or tomorrow)?"

_____

_____

_____

Question #3: When was the last time you had a genuine belly laugh, and why was it so funny?

_____

_____

_____

_____

_____

_____

_____

DAY 48

DATE _____ / _____ / _____

> *Our favorite attitude should be gratitude.*
>
> — ZIG ZIGLAR

Question #1: "I am grateful for_____, because _____."

_____

_____

_____

Question #2: "What am I looking forward to today (or tomorrow)?"

_____

_____

_____

Question #3: What body part or organ are you most grateful for today (e.g., your eyes because you got to see a new movie)?

_____

_____

_____

_____

_____

_____

DAY 49

DATE ____/____/____

> *Gratitude turns what we have into enough.*
>
> — AESOP

Question #1: "I am grateful for_____, because _____."

_____

_____

_____

Question #2: "What am I looking forward to today (or tomorrow)?"

_____

_____

_____

Question #3: What is a major lesson that you learned from your job?

_____

_____

_____

_____

_____

_____

_____

DAY 50

DATE ____/____/____

> *Reflect upon your present blessings, of which every man has plenty; not on your past misfortunes, of which all men have some.*
>
> — CHARLES DICKENS

Question #1: "I am grateful for_____, because _____."

_____

_____

_____

Question #2: "What am I looking forward to today (or tomorrow)?"

_____

_____

_____

Question #3: List 10 items that you take for granted and that might not be available to people in other parts of the world (e.g., clean water, electricity, etc.).

_____

_____

_____

_____

_____

_____

_____

DAY 51

> *He is a wise man who does not grieve for the things which he has not, but rejoices for those which he has.*
>
> — EPICTETUS

Question #1: "I am grateful for_____, because _____."

_____

_____

_____

Question #2: "What am I looking forward to today (or tomorrow)?"

_____

_____

_____

Question #3: Write about a recent time when a stranger did something nice for you.

_____

_____

_____

_____

_____

_____

_____

DAY 52

DATE ____/____/____

> Find the good and praise it.
>
> — ALEX HALEY

Question #1: "I am grateful for_____, because _____."

_____

_____

_____

Question #2: "What am I looking forward to today (or tomorrow)?"

_____

_____

_____

Question #3: What is the hardest thing you've had to do which led to a major personal accomplishment?

_____

_____

_____

_____

_____

_____

_____

_____

DAY 53

DATE ____/____/____

> *A moment of gratitude makes a difference in your attitude.*
>
> — BRUCE WILKINSON

Question #1: "I am grateful for_____, because _____."

_____

_____

_____

Question #2: "What am I looking forward to today (or tomorrow)?"

_____

_____

_____

Question #3: What is one aspect about your health that you're grateful for?

_____

_____

_____

_____

_____

_____

_____

_____

DAY 54

DATE ____/____/____

> *What separates privilege from entitlement is gratitude.*
>
> — BRENÉ BROWN

Question #1: "I am grateful for_____, because _____."

_____

_____

_____

Question #2: "What am I looking forward to today (or tomorrow)?"

_____

_____

_____

Question #3: Who can you count on whenever you need someone to talk to and why?

_____

_____

_____

_____

_____

_____

_____

_____

DAY 55

DATE ____/____/____

Question #1: "I am grateful for_____, because _____."

_____

_____

_____

Question #2: "What am I looking forward to today (or tomorrow)?"

_____

_____

_____

Question #3: Describe the last time you procrastinated on a task that wasn't as difficult as you thought it would be.

_____

_____

_____

_____

_____

_____

_____

_____

DAY 56

DATE ____/____/____

> When it comes to life the critical thing is whether you take
> things for granted or take them with gratitude.
>
> — G.K. CHESTERTON

Question #1: "I am grateful for_____, because _____."

_____

_____

_____

Question #2: "What am I looking forward to today (or tomorrow)?"

_____

_____

_____

Question #3: What is your favorite habit, and why it is an important part of your daily routine?

_____

_____

_____

_____

_____

_____

_____

_____

DAY 57

> *It is not joy that makes us grateful,*
> *it is gratitude that makes us joyful.*
>
> — DAVID STEINDL-RAST

Question #1: "I am grateful for_____, because _____."

_____

_____

_____

Question #2: "What am I looking forward to today (or tomorrow)?"

_____

_____

_____

Question #3: Describe a "perfect day" that you recently had.

_____

_____

_____

_____

_____

_____

_____

_____

DAY 58

DATE ____/____/____

> *Gratitude and attitude are not challenges; they are choices.*
>
> — ROBERT BRAATHE

Question #1: "I am grateful for_____, because _____."

_____

_____

_____

Question #2: "What am I looking forward to today (or tomorrow)?"

_____

_____

_____

Question #3: What is a favorite country that you've visited?

_____

_____

_____

_____

_____

_____

_____

_____

_____

DAY 59

> *We must never forget the importance of gratitude.*
>
> — ANONYMOUS

Question #1: "I am grateful for_____, because _____."

_____

_____

_____

Question #2: "What am I looking forward to today (or tomorrow)?"

_____

_____

_____

Question #3: Describe a funny YouTube video that you recently watched.

_____

_____

_____

_____

_____

_____

_____

_____

DAY 60

> *Gratitude is not only the greatest of virtues but the parent of all others.*
>
> — CICERO

Question #1: "I am grateful for_____, because _____."

_____

_____

_____

Question #2: "What am I looking forward to today (or tomorrow)?"

_____

_____

_____

Question #3: List 10 qualities you like about yourself.

_____

_____

_____

_____

_____

_____

_____

_____

_____

_____

DAY 61

DATE ____/____/____

> Feeling gratitude and not expressing it is like
> wrapping a present and not giving it.
>
> — WILLIAM ARTHUR WARD

Question #1: "I am grateful for_____, because _____."

_____

_____

_____

Question #2: "What am I looking forward to today (or tomorrow)?"

_____

_____

_____

Question #3: What is one thing you look forward to enjoying each day after work?

_____

_____

_____

_____

_____

_____

_____

DAY 62

DATE ____/____/____

What are you grateful for today?

— ANONYMOUS

Question #1: "I am grateful for_____, because _____."

_____

_____

_____

Question #2: "What am I looking forward to today (or tomorrow)?"

_____

_____

_____

Question #3: What was something you did for the first time recently?

_____

_____

_____

_____

_____

_____

_____

_____

DAY 63

DATE ____/____/____

> *We must find time to stop and thank the people*
> *who make a difference in our lives.*
>
> — JOHN F. KENNEDY

Question #1: "I am grateful for_____, because _____."

_____

_____

_____

Question #2: "What am I looking forward to today (or tomorrow)?"

_____

_____

_____

Question #3: What is what one lesson you have learned from rude people?

_____

_____

_____

_____

_____

_____

_____

DAY 64

DATE ____/____/____

> *Wear gratitude like a cloak and it will feed every corner of your life.*
>
> — RUMI

Question #1: "I am grateful for_____, because _____."

_____

_____

_____

Question #2: "What am I looking forward to today (or tomorrow)?"

_____

_____

_____

Question #3: When was the last time you had a great nap where you awoke feeling fully refreshed?

_____

_____

_____

_____

_____

_____

_____

_____

DAY 65

> *May the work of your hands be a sign of gratitude and reverence to the human condition.*
>
> — MAHATMA GANDHI

Question #1: "I am grateful for_____, because _____."

_____

_____

_____

Question #2: "What am I looking forward to today (or tomorrow)?"

_____

_____

_____

Question #3: Shower or bath? Which do you prefer and why?

_____

_____

_____

_____

_____

_____

_____

_____

DAY 66

> *The deepest craving of human nature is the need to be appreciated.*
>
> — WILLIAM JAMES

Question #1: "I am grateful for_____, because _____."

_____

_____

_____

Question #2: "What am I looking forward to today (or tomorrow)?"

_____

_____

_____

Question #3: Write about a time where you felt coura-
geous.

_____

_____

_____

_____

_____

_____

_____

_____

DAY 67

DATE ____/____/____

Question #1: "I am grateful for_____, because _____."

_____

_____

_____

Question #2: "What am I looking forward to today (or tomorrow)?"

_____

_____

_____

Question #3: What are a few ways you can appreciate your health whenever you're sick?

_____

_____

_____

_____

_____

_____

_____

DAY 68

DATE ____/____/____

Question #1: "I am grateful for_____, because _____."

_____

_____

_____

Question #2: "What am I looking forward to today (or tomorrow)?"

_____

_____

_____

Question #3: What is a favorite drink that you like to enjoy each day?

_____

_____

_____

_____

_____

_____

_____

_____

DAY 69

> *Gratitude is a duty which ought to be paid,*
> *but which none have a right to expect.*
>
> — JEAN-JACQUES ROUSSEAU

Question #1: "I am grateful for_____, because _____."

_____

_____

_____

Question #2: "What am I looking forward to today (or tomorrow)?"

_____

_____

_____

Question #3: Who has forgiven you for a mistake you've made in the past?

_____

_____

_____

_____

_____

_____

_____

_____

DAY 70

DATE ____/____/____

Question #1: "I am grateful for_____, because _____."

_____

_____

_____

Question #2: "What am I looking forward to today (or tomorrow)?"

_____

_____

_____

Question #3: List 10 things you have now that you didn't have five years ago.

_____

_____

_____

_____

_____

_____

_____

_____

DAY 71

DATE ____/____/____

> *When I started counting my blessings, my whole life turned around.*
>
> — WILLIE NELSON

Question #1: "I am grateful for_____, because _____."

_____

_____

_____

Question #2: "What am I looking forward to today (or tomorrow)?"

_____

_____

_____

Question #3: What aspects of your job do you enjoy the most?

_____

_____

_____

_____

_____

_____

_____

DAY 72

DATE ____/____/____

> *We often take for granted the very things that most deserve our gratitude.*
>
> — CYNTHIA OZICK

Question #1: "I am grateful for_____, because _____."

_____

_____

_____

Question #2: "What am I looking forward to today (or tomorrow)?"

_____

_____

_____

Question #3: What is a positive aspect that you can learn from one of your negative qualities (e.g., being anxious means you're really good at planning things out)?

_____

_____

_____

_____

_____

_____

_____

DAY 73

DATE ____/____/____

> *Enough is a feast.*
>
> — BUDDHIST PROVERB

Question #1: "I am grateful for_____, because _____."

_____

_____

_____

Question #2: "What am I looking forward to today (or tomorrow)?"

_____

_____

_____

Question #3: What are a few aspects of modern technology that you love?

_____

_____

_____

_____

_____

_____

_____

_____

DAY 74

DATE ____ / ____ / ____

> *The way to develop the best that is in a person is by appreciation and encouragement.*
>
> — CHARLES SCHWAB

Question #1: "I am grateful for_____, because _____."

_____

_____

_____

Question #2: "What am I looking forward to today (or tomorrow)?"

_____

_____

_____

Question #3: What is a great recipe you've prepared that others rave about?

_____

_____

_____

_____

_____

_____

_____

_____

DAY 75

> We can choose to be grateful no matter what.
>
> — DIETER F. UCHTDORF

Question #1: "I am grateful for_____, because _____."

_____

_____

_____

Question #2: "What am I looking forward to today (or tomorrow)?"

_____

_____

_____

Question #3: Describe a recent time when you truly felt at peace.

_____

_____

_____

_____

_____

_____

_____

_____

DAY 76

DATE _____/_____/_____

> *Let us be grateful to the people who make us happy; they are the charming gardeners who make our souls blossom.*
>
> — MARCEL PROUST

Question #1: "I am grateful for_____, because _____."

_____

_____

_____

Question #2: "What am I looking forward to today (or tomorrow)?"

_____

_____

_____

Question #3: What is your favorite quote or bit of wisdom that you like to frequently share with others?

_____

_____

_____

_____

_____

_____

_____

_____

DAY 77

> *A sense of blessedness comes from a change of heart,*
> *not from more blessings.*
>
> — MASON COOLEY

Question #1: "I am grateful for_____, because _____."

_____

_____

_____

Question #2: "What am I looking forward to today (or tomorrow)?"

_____

_____

_____

Question #3: What is your favorite sports team? Describe a cherished memory you have when cheering for this team.

_____

_____

_____

_____

_____

_____

_____

_____

DAY 78

DATE ____/____/____

> *The best way to pay for a lovely moment is to enjoy it.*
>
> — RICHARD BACH

Question #1: "I am grateful for_____, because _____."

_____

_____

_____

Question #2: "What am I looking forward to today (or tomorrow)?"

_____

_____

_____

Question #3: Are you a morning person or a night owl? What do you love most about this part of the day?

_____

_____

_____

_____

_____

_____

_____

DAY 79

DATE ____/____/____

> *Thankfulness may consist merely of words. Gratitude is shown in acts.*
>
> — HENRI FREDERIC AMIEL

Question #1: "I am grateful for_____, because _____."

_____

_____

_____

Question #2: "What am I looking forward to today (or tomorrow)?"

_____

_____

_____

Question #3: What is the last thank you note you've received, and why?

_____

_____

_____

_____

_____

_____

_____

_____

DAY 80

DATE ____/____/____

> *I was complaining that I had no shoes till
> I met a man who had no feet.*
>
> — CONFUCIUS

Question #1: "I am grateful for_____, because _____."

_____

_____

_____

Question #2: "What am I looking forward to today (or tomorrow)?"

_____

_____

_____

Question #3: List 10 of your favorite possessions.

_____

_____

_____

_____

_____

_____

_____

_____

_____

_____

DAY 81

> *Giving is an expression of gratitude for our blessings.*
>
> — LAURA ARRILLAGA-ANDREESSEN

Question #1: "I am grateful for_____, because _____."

_____

_____

_____

Question #2: "What am I looking forward to today (or tomorrow)?"

_____

_____

_____

Question #3: What is a small win that you accomplished in the past 24 hours?

_____

_____

_____

_____

_____

_____

_____

_____

DAY 82

DATE ____/ ____/ ____

> *Be grateful for what you have, and work hard for what you don't have.*
>
> — ANONYMOUS

Question #1: "I am grateful for_____, because _____."

_____

_____

_____

Question #2: "What am I looking forward to today (or tomorrow)?"

_____

_____

_____

Question #3: Describe one thing that you like about your daily commute to work.

_____

_____

_____

_____

_____

_____

_____

_____

DAY 83

DATE ____/____/____

> *It is only with gratitude that life becomes rich.*
>
> — DEITRICH BONHEIFFER

Question #1: "I am grateful for_____, because _____."

_____

_____

_____

Question #2: "What am I looking forward to today (or tomorrow)?"

_____

_____

_____

Question #3: What is a personal viewpoint that positively defines you as a person?

_____

_____

_____

_____

_____

_____

_____

DAY 84

DATE ____/____/____

> *We can complain because rose bushes have thorns, or rejoice because thorns have roses.*
>
> — ALPHONSE KARR

Question #1: "I am grateful for_____, because _____."

_____

_____

_____

Question #2: "What am I looking forward to today (or tomorrow)?"

_____

_____

_____

Question #3: Describe an experience that was painful but made you a stronger person.

_____

_____

_____

_____

_____

_____

_____

_____

DAY 85

> *Learn to be thankful for what you already have,*
> *while you pursue all that you want.*
>
> — JIM ROHN

Question #1: "I am grateful for_____, because _____."

_____

_____

_____

Question #2: "What am I looking forward to today (or tomorrow)?"

_____

_____

_____

Question #3: What is your favorite season, and what do you like about it?

_____

_____

_____

_____

_____

_____

_____

DAY 86

DATE ____/____/____

> *May the gratitude in my heart kiss all the universe.*
>
> — HAFIZ

Question #1: "I am grateful for_____, because _____."

_____

_____

_____

Question #2: "What am I looking forward to today (or tomorrow)?"

_____

_____

_____

Question #3: What makes you beautiful?

_____

_____

_____

_____

_____

_____

_____

_____

_____

DAY 87

DATE ____/____/____

> *Humor is mankind's greatest blessing.*
>
> — MARK TWAIN

Question #1: "I am grateful for_____, because _____."

_____

_____

_____

Question #2: "What am I looking forward to today (or tomorrow)?"

_____

_____

_____

Question #3: What are you most looking forward to this week?

_____

_____

_____

_____

_____

_____

_____

_____

DAY 88

DATE ____/____/____

> *Showing gratitude is one of the simplest yet most powerful things humans can do for each other.*
>
> — RANDY RAUSCH

Question #1: "I am grateful for_____, because _____."

_____

_____

_____

Question #2: "What am I looking forward to today (or tomorrow)?"

_____

_____

_____

Question #3: What is an app or piece of technology that you use every day that adds value to your life?

_____

_____

_____

_____

_____

_____

_____

DAY 89

DATE ____/____/____

> *If the only prayer you said in your whole life was "thank you" that would suffice.*
>
> — MEISTER ECKHART

Question #1: "I am grateful for_____, because _____."

_____

_____

_____

Question #2: "What am I looking forward to today (or tomorrow)?"

_____

_____

_____

Question #3: What makes you happy to be alive?

_____

_____

_____

_____

_____

_____

_____

_____

DAY 90

DATE ____/____/____

> *It's not happiness that brings us gratitude.*
> *It's gratitude that brings us happiness.*
>
> — ANONYMOUS

Question #1: "I am grateful for_____, because _____."

_____

_____

_____

Question #2: "What am I looking forward to today (or tomorrow)?"

_____

_____

_____

Question #3: List 10 things you like about your job or work-place.

_____

_____

_____

_____

_____

_____

_____

_____

Final Thoughts on Gratitude

Congratulations on completing
The 90-Day Gratitude Journal.

You have dedicated the last ninety days to focusing on positivity, instead of surrounding yourself with negativity. Even if you've only journaled for a few minutes daily, you have discovered what it's like to recognize the good in the world.

Embracing gratitude can have a transformative effect on your life. As mentioned before, learning how to be more grateful will:

- Increase your happiness.
- Improve your mental health.
- Allow you to savor every positive experience.
- Help you cope with major life challenges.
- Create a sense of resilience in how you approach challenging experiences.
- Boost your self-esteem.
- Foster empathy for others.
- Provide a better night's sleep.
- Strengthen both your personal and romantic relationships.

After journaling for the past ninety days, you've probably experienced many of the benefits of gratitude. Not only is it a great habit that improves your life, it can also have a positive spillover effect on the people around you.

Now, we encourage you to frequently reread this journal—at least once a month. This practice will act as a reminder about all the amazing things that you have *right now*—not in some distant, faraway future.

Finally, we would love to hear about your experience with this journal, and which prompts you found most useful. If you'd like to share your thoughts feel free to email us at sjcott@developgoodhabits.com or support@barriedavenport.com

Thanks for investing both your time and money in *The 90-Day Gratitude Journal.*

We hope you enjoyed the journey of discovering unique ways to apply gratitude your daily life.

Cheers,

S.J. Scott
Barrie Davenport

Works Cited

[1] https://www.health.harvard.edu/newsletter_article/in-praise-of-gratitude

[2] Seligman, M.; Steen, T.A.; Park, N. and Peterson, C. (2005). "Positive psychology
progress: Empirical validation of interventions," American Psychologist, 60:410-421

[3] The How of Happiness: A New Approach to Getting the Life You Want by Sonja Lyubomirsky

[4] Thanks! How Practicing Gratitude Can Make You Happier by Dr. Robert Emmon

[5] https://www.psychologytoday.com/blog/minding-the-body/201111/how-gratitude-helps-you-sleep-night

[6] Willpower: Rediscovering the Human Strength by Roy F. Baumeister and John Tierney.

[7] https://lifehacker.com/281626/jerry-seinfelds-productivity-secret

[8] Seligman, M.; Steen, T.A.; Park, N. and Peterson, C. (2005). "Positive psychology progress: Empirical validation of interventions," American Psychologist, 60:410-421.

Made in the USA
Coppell, TX
09 March 2020